SECONDS TO SURVIVE

USING C.A.L.M. TO NAVIGATE POLICE STOPS
WITH CONFIDENCE

COREY V. TAYLOR SR.

Table Of Contents

INTRODUCTION

Over 50,000 people are pulled over each day by U.S. law enforcement. For most, it is a minor inconvenience. But for some—particularly people of color—a routine traffic stop can become a life-or-death situation. This book is not about fear; it is about empowerment. It is about being equipped with the mindset and method that can increase your chances of surviving encounters with police.

I created the acronym C.A.L.M. to teach a practical, step-by-step approach to traffic stops and police interactions. C.A.L.M. stands for:

- Comply – Follow lawful commands.
- Answer – Respond clearly and respectfully.
- Listen – Pay attention to instructions and context.

- Move On – Safely exit the encounter and understand what comes next.

Each of these principles is rooted in real-world events—tragic losses, close calls, and successful outcomes. Our goal is not to blame victims or excuse misconduct, but to provide you with tools that improve your chances in critical moments.

Whether you're a parent talking to your teen, a driver preparing for the unexpected, or simply a concerned citizen, *Seconds to Survive* is your guide to navigating the thin line between law and life. Because during a police stop, you may only have seconds to make the right decision.

CHAPTER 1: COMPLY – THE FIRST STEP TOWARD CONTROL

What It Means:

To comply is not to submit blindly—it is to follow lawful orders to de-escalate a situation. Compliance shows that you are not a threat.

Compliance is not a sign of weakness or fear. True compliance is an act of strength—it is the use of intelligence and restraint to ensure you walk away safely. When a police officer gives a command, especially during a traffic stop, the safest course of action is to comply first and contest later. Even if the stop feels unfair, unsafe, or unjust, staying alive must be the priority.

Real Life Example:

Philando Castile complied by informing the officer that he had a legal firearm, but his subsequent movement led to fatal confusion. This tragic case highlights thc importance of how you comply—with calmness, clarity, and without sudden motions.

Real Life Example:

Army Lt. Caron Nazario was pulled over at night in Virginia while in uniform. He chose to drive a short distance to a well-lit gas station for safety—an action within his rights. However, when he did not immediately exit his vehicle as ordered, officers escalated the situation with pepper spray and aggressive commands. Had Nazario calmly explained his intentions while keeping his hands visible and complying step by step, the situation might have been de-escalated more quickly. His actions were not wrong, but the perceived resistance heightened tensions.

Real Life Example:

Jacob Blake was involved in a domestic incident during which officers attempted to detain him. He walked away from the officers and attempted to enter a vehicle, leading to a shooting that occurred in front of his children. While the facts of the case remain disputed, had he complied with the initial commands and remained verbally engaged instead of moving away, the outcome might have been different. Compliance does not guarantee justice, but non-compliance can increase the risk of escalation.

Real Life Example:

Michael Dean, a father from Texas, was shot during a traffic stop for a minor violation. He moved his hands in a way the officer perceived as non-compliant, though witnesses later disputed the level of threat. The investigation highlighted a lack of clear commands and communication. This case underscores the importance of compliance paired with vocal acknowledgment—such as saying, “My hands are on the wheel, officer”—to help clarify your intent during high-stress encounters.

Real Life Example:

Shawn Montague, a teenager in New Jersey, was stopped on suspicion of vehicle theft. He fully complied, even placing his phone on the dashboard and narrating his actions: 'Reaching for license now.' Bodycam footage showed how his deliberate and clear compliance led to a calm and respectful interaction, despite the tense circumstances.

Case Law:

Terry v. Ohio (1968) established that officers can stop and frisk a person based on reasonable suspicion. Compliance does not mean agreeing with the stop—it means surviving it.

Graham v. Connor (1989) is another cornerstone case, holding that an officer's use of force must be “objectively reasonable” under the Fourth Amendment. Reasonableness is judged from the perspective of the officer at the scene, not with the benefit of hindsight. This underscores the importance of compliance: if actions are perceived as threatening—even mistakenly—it can legally justify the use of force.

Reflection Questions:

1. Think of a time when you were frustrated or scared in a public setting.
2. How might your behavior in that moment be misinterpreted by someone who does not know your intentions?
3. How can you prepare yourself (mentally and physically) to remain calm and compliant, even if the situation feels unfair?

CHAPTER 2: ANSWER – SPEAK SMART, STAY SAFE

What It Means:

Answer questions clearly and respectfully. You have rights—but know when to speak and when to remain silent. Law enforcement officers are trained to assess threats quickly, and how you respond verbally can shape the outcome of the stop. Answering questions does not mean confessing; it means communicating.

Answering truthfully and calmly can often be the difference between receiving a simple citation and facing a prolonged detainment. It demonstrates cooperation without submission and gives the officer less reason to escalate.

Real Life Example:

Sandra Bland asserted her rights during a minor traffic stop. Her refusal to answer certain questions escalated tensions. While legally permissible, the fallout was devastating. Had there been clearer communication, her situation might have unfolded differently.

Real Life Example:

John Lewis, a young man, was stopped by police in Georgia and asked if he knew why. Instead of becoming defensive, he replied, "I may have rolled through that stop sign back there." The officer confirmed that was the reason and appreciated his honesty. The stop ended with a warning. John's respectful and straightforward answer defused tension and humanized the interaction.

Real Life Example:

Diamond Reynolds, who was with Philando Castile during the infamous Minnesota traffic stop, recorded the aftermath with remarkable composure. She answered the officers' questions clearly and respectfully, even as chaos unfolded around her. Her responses helped clarify the events for the public and investigators and supported her narrative that Philando had attempted to comply.

Real Life Example:

Jordan Matthews, a college student in Alabama, was pulled over for a broken taillight. When asked if he had any weapons or illegal substances, he admitted to carrying a small pocketknife and handed it over calmly. His honesty and calm tone put the officer at ease. Jordan received a citation and was allowed to leave. His composed and straightforward responses showed that he had nothing to hide and respected the process.

Real Life Example:

Leah Thompson, a nurse from Chicago, was pulled over for a minor lane violation. When asked where she was headed, she calmly explained that she was leaving her shift at the hospital and offered her ID. The officer let her go with a warning. Her calm and honest explanation instantly built credibility.

Real Life Example:

Carlos Rivera, a construction worker in Arizona, was stopped in a neighborhood where he did not live. When asked what he was doing in the area, he simply explained that he was working a late shift on a nearby home and showed photos of the job on his phone. His honest, proactive response helped de-escalate suspicion.

Do's and Don'ts:

Do:

- Provide license, registration, and insurance without hesitation.
- Answer basic questions clearly and concisely.
- Be truthful, especially when asked about weapons or documentation.
- Use phrases like "Yes, officer," or "I understand," to show cooperation.

Don't:

- Lie or providing false information can be a criminal offense.
- Argue or try to 'talk your way out' with emotional language.
- Refuse to answer at all unless you are invoking your right to remain silent—and even then, do so calmly and clearly.

Legal Insight:

Miranda v. Arizona (1966) gave rise to the famous Miranda Rights, including the right to remain silent. However, these rights are read only after an arrest has been made. During a traffic stop, basic questions about your identity and vehicle documents must still be answered under most state laws.

Being honest during a stop is not about incriminating yourself; it is about protecting yourself. Your answers create a record of calm, cooperative behavior that could make all the difference—whether in court or in the moment.

Reflection Questions:

1. What are some questions you might be asked during a traffic stop, and how would you answer them in a calm, truthful way?
2. What is the difference between answering honestly and volunteering unnecessary information? Where is the line?

CHAPTER 3: LISTEN – HEAR WHAT'S SAID (AND WHAT'S NOT)

What It Means:

Listening during a police stop is more than just hearing words—it involves actively understanding the officer's instructions, tone, and body language. Listening helps reduce misunderstandings that can quickly escalate tension.

When you listen carefully, you demonstrate respect and cooperation. It also gives you the opportunity to catch crucial information, such as why you are being stopped, what the officer expects from you, and when you are free to leave. Being an active listener means responding appropriately to commands and showing that you are engaged in the process—not resisting.

Listening is not passive; it requires focus and patience, even if you feel nervous or frustrated. Your ability to absorb and process what the officer is saying can change the entire dynamic of the encounter.

Real Life Example:

Trayvon Martin's father, Tracy Martin, shared in interviews that his son was told to stop and listen by a community watch volunteer before the fatal confrontation. The failure to fully listen and understand the situation quickly escalated into violence. Although he was not stopped by the police, this case underscores how critical active listening and communication are in potentially life-threatening encounters.

Real Life Example:

Brandon Smith was pulled over in California for a broken taillight. He listened attentively as the officer calmly explained the reason for the stop and the steps he needed to take next. When the officer asked Brandon to step out and perform a field sobriety test, Brandon remained composed, listened carefully to the instructions, and followed them precisely. Because he complied promptly, the stop concluded peacefully, and Brandon was free to leave with just a warning.

Legal Context:

Listening closely aligns with the "objective reasonableness" standard established in *Graham v. Connor* (1989), where officers evaluate situations based on what they perceive at that moment. If a person fails to listen to or understand an officer's commands, it may be considered non-compliance, which can legally justify escalation.

Moreover, courts often assess whether a person's failure to listen contributed to confusion or resistance. This is why understanding and adhering to verbal commands is crucial for both safety and legal protection.

Dos and Don'ts for Listening:

Do:

- Stay focused on what the officer is saying.
- Confirm understanding by nodding or calmly repeating instructions if unsure.
- Keep your hands visible and avoid distractions like your phone.
- Ask for clarification politely if you do not understand a command.

Don't:

- Interrupt or talk over the officer.
- Ignore commands or respond with sarcasm.
- Assume you know what is going to happen next without listening.
- Become defensive or argumentative if you disagree with what is said.

Reflection Questions:

1. How do you usually respond when you are nervous or anxious?
2. How can improving your listening skills help you in high-stress situations like a traffic stop?
3. What are some strategies you can practice improving your active listening during tense moments?

CHAPTER 4: MOVE ON – THE AFTERMATH AND THE BIGGER PICTURE

What It Means:

"**Move on**" means ending the encounter safely without escalating the situation further. It involves recognizing when the interaction is over or when it's time to comply fully and exit the scene. The goal is not to give up your rights but to prioritize survival so you can fight another day through the proper channels, such as courts, legal advocacy, or public awareness.

Walking away with dignity and safety preserves your ability to seek justice later. Reacting impulsively or challenging an officer during a stop can increase danger and reduce your chances of a favorable outcome. **"Moving on"** is a strategic decision, not surrender.

Real Life Example:

Philando Castile's girlfriend, Diamond Reynolds, famously recorded the aftermath of the fatal shooting on live video. While Philando complied during the stop, Diamond's quick decision to remain calm, speak directly to the camera, and avoid escalating tensions with the officers helped preserve crucial evidence and brought national attention to the incident. Her ability to "move on" safely after the immediate threat saved her life and had a powerful impact.

Real Life Example:

Eric Garner repeatedly said, "I can't breathe," during his arrest for allegedly selling untaxed cigarettes. Although he was resisting, the failure to effectively "move on" (comply fully and seek justice afterward) tragically cost him his life. This case highlights the vital importance of knowing when to stop resisting—even in unjust situations—to protect yourself physically.

Legal Context:

The right to due process means you can challenge unlawful stops, excessive force, or discrimination—but only after the stop, not during it. The Fourth Amendment protects against unreasonable searches and seizures, but courts generally do not look favorably on resistance or refusal during the encounter.

Cases like *Tennessee v. Garner* (1985) establish limits on the use of deadly force against fleeing suspects, but even then, complying and cooperating during a stop reduces the risk of such force being used.

Dos and Don'ts for Moving On:

Do:

- Wait for the officer's signal that you are free to leave.
- Gather all necessary documents quietly and hand them over promptly.

- Stay calm, thank the officer if appropriate, and exit without haste.
- Use your phone or recorder only after the interaction ends if safe.

Don't:

- Drive away before being told you can leave—it is illegal and can escalate the situation.
- Argue or demand explanations on the spot.
- Physically resist or make sudden movements when told to "move on."
- Forget that you have legal recourse after the stop—your voice matters outside the encounter.

Reflection Questions:

1. How can practicing patience and self-control during a stop empower you in the long term?
2. What steps can you take after a stop to document and report if you believe your rights were violated?

CHAPTER 5: THE DO'S AND DON'TS OF TRAFFIC STOPS – YOUR SURVIVAL CHECKLIST

What It Means:

Knowing what to do—and what to avoid—during a traffic stop can be the difference between a routine encounter and a dangerous situation. This chapter distills essential survival tactics into clear, actionable advice. These guidelines are designed to keep you safe, protect your rights, and reduce the risk of misunderstandings.

The Do's:

- Always keep your hands visible, preferably on the steering wheel. This reduces the officer's anxiety and shows you are not a threat.

- Provide your license, registration, and proof of insurance promptly when asked. Delays can be misinterpreted as suspicious.
- Remain polite and respectful, even if you feel the stop is unfair. Your tone and demeanor influence the officer's reaction.
- Inform the officer if you have a weapon in the vehicle and have the legal right to carry it. Always do this calmly and clearly before reaching for anything.
- Comply fully with lawful commands, including staying in the vehicle unless asked to exit.
- Record the stop if you can safely do so without escalating tension. Make sure the recording is visible to the officer.

The Don'ts:

- Do not reach suddenly or make unexpected movements, as sudden motions can be perceived as threats.
- Do not argue, raise your voice, or use aggressive language. Even if you disagree, keep your cool.
- Do not refuse to provide documentation unless you are invoking your legal right to remain silent; even then, do so calmly.
- Do not exit the vehicle unless asked. Getting out without permission can escalate the situation.
- Do not attempt to flee or resist physically, as this can lead to the use of force and criminal charges.
- Do not lie or provide false documents, as this can lead to arrest or harsher penalties.

Real Life Example:

Sandra Bland's traffic stops in Texas became a tragic case study after a minor violation escalated. Her refusal to comply with orders and to exit the vehicle peacefully led to her arrest and subsequent death in jail. This heartbreaking example illustrates the risks of non-compliance and underscores the importance of following proper procedures.

Real-Life Example:

Jerome Adams, pulled over for speeding in New York, followed all procedures by remaining calm, promptly providing his documents, and answering questions respectfully. The officer issued a warning, and the stop ended quickly. Jerome later credited his calm approach as key to a peaceful encounter.

Legal Context:

Miranda v. Arizona (1966) protects your right against self-incrimination but primarily applies after an arrest. During a stop, you are generally required to identify yourself in most states. Refusing to comply with lawful requests can result in lawful detention or arrest.

Pennsylvania v. Mimms (1977) established that officers may order drivers out of their vehicles during a traffic stop for safety reasons without violating the Fourth Amendment. Exiting the vehicle without being asked can be misinterpreted as resistance.

Reflection Questions:

1. How can you mentally rehearse the Do's and Don'ts to prepare for an unexpected traffic stop?
2. What changes can you make in your communication style to ensure respectful and clear interactions with officers?

CHAPTER 6: SURVIVING IS THE WIN – FINAL REFLECTIONS

When the flashing lights fade and the stop is over, survival is the victory. There is no prize for arguing your rights on the roadside, no medal for debating the law with a badge. The real win lies in going home alive and empowered.

This book has equipped you with the C.A.L.M. method: Comply, Answer, Listen, Move On. You have read stories of heartbreak and triumph, of pain and perseverance. You have seen how a moment of composure can change everything. The lessons in these pages are not hypothetical—they are life-tested. And they are yours to carry.

Our mission with *Seconds to Survive* is not to instill fear but to foster preparation. You now have tools to protect your life, your dignity, and your future. In a world where things can go wrong in the blink of an eye, your calm might be your greatest weapon.

To the young person who fears the siren. To the parents who worry every time their child gets behind the wheel. To the teacher, pastor, mentor, neighbor—share this knowledge. Spread it like armor. Let these seconds be sacred.

Because surviving is not surrender. It is strategy.

And sometimes, surviving is enough.

Final Reflection Questions:

1. What changes will you make in how you respond to law enforcement moving forward?
2. Who in your life needs this information—and how will you share it?

Stay calm. Stay smart. Stay alive.

www.ingramcontent.com/pod-product-compliance
Lightning Source LLC
LaVergne TN
LVHW022325200926
848481LV00004B/1436